The Triumph of Sorrow:
A Lover of Longing

poems by

Uzomah Ugwu

Finishing Line Press
Georgetown, Kentucky

The Triumph of Sorrow:
A Lover of Longing

ACKNOWLEDGMENTS

Minute Magazine, "Lit parties by the ocean" (2019)
Medium," Lighting", 2021
Medium, "Imperfect Timing" 2022
Medium, "If It Had Only Begun" 2022

Publisher: Leah Huete de Maines
Editor: Christen Kincaid
Cover Art: Dream Soldier acrylic, Uzomah Ugwu
Author Photo: Charles Ugwu
Cover Design: Elizabeth Maines McCleavy

Order online: www.finishinglinepress.com
also available on amazon.com

Author inquiries and mail orders:
Finishing Line Press
PO Box 1626
Georgetown, Kentucky 40324
USA

Table of Contents

*This book is dedicated to my father and mother,
who never stopped believing in me.*

Wrapped in Your Tears

Walked over your tears once more. Perched at the door with bags tilted by your side. Said you left the store in a rush to find what you couldn't ignore or fix. Close to a crawl, you moved across the floor so small. Grabbing the wall like you would fall, slip and dissolve. You said I was not to be won just be the one for you. Gentle eyes of yours looked in me till I bled all over my body. Became wrapped in your words to heal the wounds, drank your tears like broken truth. But I couldn't stay, ran midway crushed the eggs on the way out knowing you loved me more than it was worth.

Fences Lost

Cornfields put up better
Then fences lost among the light
But the darkness feeds us faster

Started off a disaster, unable to turn off
The sound crowded streets heard
With cars that didn't move
Fought so hard to have no beginnings
Now falling apart with no end

Used to eat red jellybeans on Thursday
When reality hurt the most
Filled with rotten teeth
Shown in words too weak to speak
That no one wants a repeat of a love
I can not find nor deny

Out of Mind Gone with Touch

Strangers like you make me blind
Unable to be with dreams in my mind
What a touch by you was like on nights
Where stars licked the moon
We talked and laughed about nothing new

Soft rushed thoughts that couldn't
make this up
Laid by your body to stay warm
It's how you betrayed my being
that made it all cold
But it felt good
You kept orbiting around me like
you knew my planet
But did you absorb any of my sentences
Look for what I wanted to say and didn't
That formed you were the one

With a force we exchanged gentle stares
from the beauty
In the eyes where lies are shown
That there was a you and me

Best Not to Know You

Missed you long enough to know
It is best I do not know you

Summer nights with bugs that light
The moon between me and you
Far from the end too close
To be friends without a comprise

You said everything would be alright
As your hand slide down my back, I don't
Wish for that moment back where your fingers
Were so close to unhooking my bra
Or that we were still friends
Or were we really that
Now hours just added
up to something different

To love being all we had to
maybe show this indifference
In the morning nothing more in the future had promise
But your lips touching mine and making
it hard for me to refrain
Then it becomes best not to you know

If It Had Only Begun

He would not let his emotions
Be shared with me
He shut down before we had miles to go
He said he could be the one for me
But he had these things he couldn't let go
I cried enough to fill an
abandon river like I would his heart
When I started to weep like a Willow Tree
I thought I had come too far to go back
but he wanted me to go and fast just
like in a hurry he said he had found me at last
The greatest love we never would have
I began to wonder why they said
happily ever after when I know
This loss ahead of reality would
be a dark fantasy he wished he never had
As for me I ached in how he
thought he wasn't the man for me
like my advances were just flashes in a pan,
and how I was traveling off the
words he drove into my heart
Only to crash
He became the best part of me
I was not meant to have
While I was still his dream girl
because I was open with my flaws as well as my claws
My beauty still would taunt him
Like his mind would still haunt me
I found love at the wrong hour
So the days went on for weeks
without me, and the months forgot
I may have been in a love
that had so much to offer
if it had only begun

Left Past

Can't leave the past because
It would mean forgetting you.

Unlike leaves dropping from trees,
knowing is certain
To return and bloom in another spring,
a strong echo with a sense
To be afraid with seconds that make up
minutes where I was something to you

On a wooden path, splinters running through my
Hands to my feet but nothing cuts me like what
You said in the leaves that speak loudly behind you

Went to the store, knocking down isles
with regret and unrequited love
I spent on you instead
on chips and sugar free gum
can't buy you back or exchange
what still weighs on my soul

my heart still heavy with each step
all in my mind, tunes find melodies
that should forget you

Piles of Needles

Mountains wrapped in string filled with
Tops spinning off of things we couldn't see
Most hope to know what spring and love truly brings
I found love in arms that weren't filled with promises to be mine

Tiger's eyes watch while the lies pile on like needles in the hay
Names called but not one said for me so I was abandoned in vain
Walking away was easy because you didn't feel so I fell in parts of
myself

I wanted to be loved but was pushed over by moons shinning too soon
On nights I knew it wasn't right that you weren't my baby and that was
fine

Imperfect Timing

Troubled and around
Around and round an answer
Reserved for years we did not

Deserve to come so late in life
Should have stayed yours and young in
Those moments not lost but so found
Where most people lose things between
The seats in movie theaters

We were each other's features where we snuck in
Each other's eyes no need for stolen tickets we fostered
A look in our eyes that no time

Passing would forget or would be affected by it
sitting while living my life
away waiting for a love I
searched for blind without knowing I had it so near

Nothing ticked not even my watch to alert
Time had gone by or arrived at another hour

Life moved us in directions that
would move us together
only to drive us apart
Which was maybe an indication
we were only perfect
when we were young
Or the timing was off

when we returned to the love
 that found us
for we became old too soon
Troubled by a love that remains

I sit in movie theaters alone waiting for
the credits like I wait for a reason
to again say your name

Misplaced Whispers

Heard whispers for a thousand years
Tall fountains held my tears while birds
Took baths in this unfinished pain

Heard your name fly back as it had
A place in the sky where angels hid
But could not deny you were there nor
Could the sky misplace the stars in my eyes

I felt your reasons why but
couldn't understand
Your goodbye
Lifeless let alone I get lost in
how I can't feel
Your face press against mine
So I lose myself in the time I don't have
You for myself

Lavender and Peppermints

He rode on her pearl-like skin
But missed a turn, though she had enough
Stars stirring and lighting her up to find his way
In the wrong part of the afternoon

Her ship had a another destination; he was a stop
Not a final place where her coat would hang on the wall
Where her heart would rest, but it was nice there where he was.

She saw him be what he never knew of himself
Riding on empty luck
Searching for a hand was not enough anymore
He will never forget not being the man she needed
That stands up in time

They fell in just to have nothing in a light that flashed shades of blue
On her eyes that couldn't look up
He said she would sail his way one day again soon
And if not he would risk it to return to her where ever she went

But this rough afternoon when her pearl-like skin
Was all he wanted to be familiar with and the hint of lavender and
Peppermints he smelled when he went to kiss her
With the clock hitting a hard six on the hour,
He knows the only road he will miss taking is to the dock that
Leads back to a ride with her that he only wanted to know best.

A Polished Her

He made a turn, two lefts
Forgot what was right

His palms collapsed forming
Tight fists of regret

Unsure what to fight
Laughed out of sight

Holes in the curtains
Looked through only

To be seen through
One quick moment

Took his bliss
Misery kissed him

On the forehead
He bowed with two steps

Past winter he accepted her
Like splinters, he felt when he sat

Down on picnic tables in spring
He loved parts of her that weren't finished

He promised to polish her
Bring her a love in her

she once couldn't find
but he didn't

Lighting

Kisses of lighting striking on the cusps of a throbbing air
Sending rooftops off of the frames to homes that can not stand alone

Too close and far away to find a way to overcome these rumbles of
emotions
Locked in chests of lovers past present and future sent

Rushed by glitter filled devotion sparkling in red like the blood
Emptying out of pools in the season where love was found

To sustain this feeling that contains all other thoughts locked
In a shed with tools in it, yet none can be found to fix this

There are a few rules to all of this simply leave It or love it
either way you are alone in a room with the ceiling gone

With the sky falling down on your heavy breathes aching on
Thinking of a time past you can not forget at a desk

Sitting in a chair with a wheel missing so you are barely able to
Spin or twist any decisions into the air rather than keep them
suffocated

in still thoughts of your on and off beating heart
Since having that last kiss of lighting striking your lips

My Body Spoke His Name

You spoke my
name having
My body echo
your intentions
When your hands
raised the hairs

Left on my body
up not cut from
The most recent shave
Wanted to hide
To be perfect and
smooth for you

For you to slide with ease
not feel this morning dew
You championed my love
With tight touches you applied

My desire with your tucks
and grabs and pressing of my skin
You asked for no favors
nothing in return
Just that I would not
ask if you were done.

Framed Dresses

Put you in a frame couldn't remember
Your name, loose ties
On my dress knew your hands well
Still hung up on a ride
Should not have hopped on

Dancing for hours, a need for showers
You fell on my shoulders like snow
You felt the need to get close
Close enough to know the taste
Of the corners of my lips

you liked me better without the makeup
made moves that didn't sound like goodbye
lost in a room with objects with a frame
looking on them

Off and Running Past Dawns Up in the Air

Lovers roam, teachers without
lessons forget sleep
Draw blanks across the stars

In the mood but no one knows
Who you were to me
In the night full of lint
You held me close only to forget
Not even trying to reach for
what was missing
But you were on the run

Loving the dust left behind
Hoping it will collect and make up
Your design

Risks break the bank can't cash in on a mistake
Roads traveled you felt you were honest on
Ones you traveled hard
without causing despair

But so alone and awake
It was true you couldn't be the man
I wanted. you needed to be true to you
Isolated with your broken wings
Free to fly where you wanted to

Hard to Love

Felt your presence around the corners
Of stories printed on pages with the light out
Glowing at midnight on the words with you to turn
This chapter, lost on the curve of winding paths
Taken to be close to you
Cut halves of warm cookies on kitchen counters
Not as sweet as your lips echoing I am good enough

Screams of lust, terror driven thrust
Dancing on tempers filled with fever
Too old to rust, too heavy to dump

Brokedown in the form of days that you
promised the same love to her
but you loved me
rope jumping little girls
smile with teeth as white as pearls
fearing to grow up and be the second fiddle to
another girl
I went back to being a little girl
because if this is growing up
Because love isn't something
I want when I say your name

Stayed Anyway

He wasn't the one but he stayed anyway
And became one I couldn't forget

Never loved enough but tried
Now tired of the wind blowing me by

Shouts in the sky divide our house
Unwashed pants you should wear out the stains

While I talk with myself to no end with
Treasures for sale left bare, so my soul cant afford to care

I love you came too late
But I stayed anyway.

Her

His bold moves to be my side with passionate strides
Had me feeling how his mutual desire and thoughts
Had ridden into my mind till my soul was driven wild
With a heart lit with affection all this attention,
Without mentioning or catching his name
He said mine with clarity and devotion that laid out
My emotions design his focus stayed in tune
To my overflowing conversation with him,

I enjoyed in vain for someone was listening
and paying attention to my story
As if it could be published as he edited
my elements of style of this new
Found self-glory of shining confidence
and pride from some type of
Love being looked into my eyes

I felt a drop in his jaw, and his eyes shifted gears
I said what, then
he pointed and asked me if I knew
HER and as I turned, I looked and I knew
all the hers like her and the ones

He did not want to just talk to but also
touch and make a scandal into a relationship
Like lust meant trust now trapped

As the runner up I saw my exit
as well as the wounds of defeat
A moment ago, he swept me off my feet till he found
Something better a winner which was her

I excused myself, but I was far out of
his attention span to notice me anymore no longer
Lurking in front of him

I went to the bathroom where tears
should have come but it was a different
Rain that came down my cheeks
It was of shame

I couldn't compete with the hers of this world
who would actually get to know the guys
Like him by name
I just would never be her
So I left as a she instead

Borrowed Possessions

it was not supposed to be like this
it was mine that I did not let you borrow or even take
pulling at my sides is your arms and hands
with legs in stance to steal what was meant for god
or my true lovers hands you took a gift that was not meant for this
like duct tape your hand sealed the now weaken voice within

and attached your hands to my face leaving residue not suited
for the little girl in me I once knew
blocking me from screaming of how I was demanding I never
wanted it this way

torn are my clothes spread everywhere in pieces
alone in the world it seemed impossible with your
body heat over top of me yielding an act responsible
for me being out mentally while

my body lay awake in defeat with my insides
numb to the touch of your deceit
every move that I made was
an attempt to free myself
from your illegal thrust that
put me in position to forever

be unable to forget the threat
 you placed over my innocence
I wept tears so dry for my body
was now broken down to dust

When you were through
For I knew it had just begun
And that you had not finished

History

A failed occasion
Pale concerns on unconsumed minds
Broken by times of suppression
Leaving many in the fields of depression
Then the fields of spring harvest
She guessed at its resistance to be the reason
She and her people were left
behind but so much in delusion
Of the celebration when she would try past the day
That offered no remembrance to her tribe
Just a day to eat
Sweet potatoes pie other than cherry
And give thanks to the Cowboys
now a football team and little
To the people that gave them
everything to be thankful for
means nothing. They took and took
till looking at her history hurt

Jazz Notes

He sought sounds that reached to parts
Of him that he could no longer muster to hold
Rushed in a motionless silence where
he did not cease to mold the image
he long heard before
the face his heart outlined with
notes in the shape of an instrument
 were so bold and with a striking pose
reflecting that a match so harmonious
 was something he had
and now was something he lacked
he waited for the drums
to bring that sensation back
and reenlist the feelings
 of holding her back gracefully
as they would dance and
forget she had left
for a better beat

lit parties by the ocean

Everyone at   the party
with a once blossoming girl that is misdressed
With petals that colored the earth now are left to die
Deep within her eyes lies a patience gone that once
Kept the sadness at the bays of stale laughter heard for miles of her
peers

With shores drowning the sand with rain flowing into confined tides
That brought clouds laying on top
of so many armies after her hearts ambition
That got in the way of others joy especially
hers a target did she forget to not remember this
Type of pain running through and after her

She was just their toy they wound up
to make their misery fade while hers stayed on the cusps
Of a sealed door with a frozen knob
unable to be turned did they realize
The light of the moon had died on their failed nights
And failed to rise and make a mood
 so soothing which was also comprised in the broken sunlight
By unjust emotional ties to the girl who
 held the earth inside within an endless party of

Greed and pride and a lust for making
an end of lives not encouraging one to go on
That left her victimized and accustomed
to a picture frame's edges being burnt that brought
Broken lies to images already torn
 left to be open the beginning
Of ties that made touches to flattened
 truths that come as no surprise as her dreams
Fluttered She was the last one to leave a party of death
That her lonely deranged life had met
A kept soul unable to find a way to leave
An open secret floating on ghosts that
Wanted to see her life end the most

Possible Course of Action

A solution meant a conflict with
Parts of society
That inflicted with their morals
That put me in a position against my will

A choice now an abused right
Takes my self-esteem from the light

Not planned but not unwanted
Just can't find the heart

To not see a day where I can
Mange something I didn't expect
Not something I did not desire to have
Not able at the moment makes me a monster

Now a selected death
I had names flash before my eyes

Summer times at the pool
I thought I could handle you bring

You in this world as my child
But as the world tries to change my mind

Wasn't there so much in retrospective
Hanging in empty baby chairs
Sleeping in cribs but
I couldn't have you here

Not in spring, or not in fall
Will I be able to take care of you

So I say goodbye before hello
To a lost child of mine

Distorted Mental Checks

broken sunsets project twisted rays
with dim lusters of a spirit trapped, locked
and positioned to feel anything but their toes

cross examinations, basic of any ER, yet differ
for a mental check, then the judging
begins on any visible aspect that becomes
both abstract and concrete, in this being
becoming a thought far from here for those
who try to pry into sanity's intersection of action
that have come crashing so much a hospital visit
couldn't be avoided

next is a voyage into walls that absorb once loud voices
into a silence beckoning that wishes it was a choice being here

food is standard down to the calories per serving
begging nurses for a doctor rather than just taking the pills they offer
just a justification while waiting for the clock to raise eye brows of others
 with peace offerings of their insanity as a way
of conforming or a way to adhere to their customs
that will never make anything normal
stretch marks left on the mind from the pulling
never releasing, just the stressing on your being
they make you think you're the reason they are doing this to you
they never explain you are not your illness
they never explain the pain
in their distorted mental checks

Force It

Trees fell on my body
Covering me
Like decisions held in court that
Were supreme to advise what should be done
With the parts of my body without my consent

Not ready, yet don't have any pets
They say are good practice for the real thing
Not an adult in a world where people
Run like wild children on playgrounds

I decided but what did that mean
when judges had duties to fulfill
to back their outdated morals and philosophies

Not able in my mind
my body couldn't respond
It just wasn't designed for this
A child and having one

So it made no sense to force it
Now when there was no answer
To how I could do better on my own
There was no question with another person to guide while
Also losing my path fighting for the right
To choose, I keep promises to liberties
They are stomping out
I found myself lost in a rapture
Of uncertainty lacking hope
To understand why I can't do what I find is
Best. When it becomes against the law.
I lose the ability to find myself or any rest

Off Keyed Days

No song to sing
So, I found tears to cry
On an awkward holiday
Celebrating the end of
An inhumane winter
Only to enter a brittle spring
Full of future injustices blooming
these lacks of humanity filled roses
That puck you with their thorns
In the garden of endless midnights
And blank stares of the sun full of despair
Unstable gardening marks it is unable to find fertile
Soil for space needed for a new born idea to take form
And grow with the type of roots that cause
An uprising that leads into a revolution

Uzomah Ugwu is a poet/writer, curator, and multi-disciplined artist. Her poetry, writing, and art have been featured internationally in various publications, galleries, and art spaces. She is a political, social, and cultural activist. Her core focus is on human rights, mental health, animal rights, and the rights of LGBTQIA persons. She is also the managing editor and founder of Arte Realizzata..

www.ingramcontent.com/pod-product-compliance
Lightning Source LLC
Chambersburg PA
CBHW022057080426
42734CB00009B/1390